LINCOLN LOGS CREATOR

John Lloyd Wright

MEGAN BORGERT-SPANIOL

Checkerboard
Library

An Imprint of Abdo Publishing
abdobooks.com

abdobooks.com

Published by Abdo Publishing, a division of ABDO, PO Box 398166, Minneapolis, Minnesota 55439. Copyright © 2019 by Abdo Consulting Group, Inc. International copyrights reserved in all countries. No part of this book may be reproduced in any form without written permission from the publisher. Checkerboard Library™ is a trademark and logo of Abdo Publishing.

Printed in the United States of America, North Mankato, Minnesota
102018
012019

Design and Production: Mighty Media, Inc.
Editor: Katherine Hengel Frankowski
Cover Photographs: Collection of the La Jolla Historical Society (center); Mighty Media, Inc.
Interior Photographs: Alamy, p. 18; born1945/Flickr, pp. 8, 28 (left); Collection of the La Jolla Historical Society, p. 27; Courtesy Jon Granston, p. 21; Courtesy of The Strong, Rochester, New York, pp. 12, 29 (top); Courtesy of The Strong, Rochester, New York, pp. 14, 15, 19, 28 (right); Internet Archive Book Images/Flickr, p. 6; Jennifer Morrow/Flickr, p. 5; Kobbaka/Wikimedia Commons, p. 22; Library of Congress, p. 9; Mighty Media, Inc., pp. 24, 26, 29 (bottom); San Diego History Center, p. 7; Shutterstock, p. 23; Spencer Hopkins, p. 17; ©2018 HASBRO. All Rights Reserved. p. 25; Wikimedia Commons, pp. 10, 11, 13

Library of Congress Control Number: 2018948787

Publisher's Cataloging-in-Publication Data
Names: Borgert-Spaniol, Megan, author.
Title: Lincoln Logs creator: John Lloyd Wright / by Megan Borgert-Spaniol.
Other title: John Lloyd Wright
Description: Minneapolis, Minnesota : Abdo Publishing, 2019 | Series: Toy
    trailblazers set 3 | Includes online resources and index.
Identifiers: ISBN 9781532117091 (lib. bdg.) | ISBN 9781532159930 (ebook)
Subjects: LCSH: Wright, John Lloyd--Juvenile literature. | Inventors--United
    States--Biography--Juvenile literature. | Lincoln Logs (Trademark)--Juvenile
    literature. | Toymakers--Biography--Juvenile literature.
Classification: DDC 688.72092 [B]--dc23

CONTENTS

Chapter 1

BUILDING
Blocks

Lincoln Logs are wooden building blocks for kids. They were first released in 1924. Nearly 100 years later, Lincoln Logs are still popular toys! They were invented by American **architect** and toy designer John Lloyd Wright.

John was the son of Frank Lloyd Wright, a famous architect. Frank had a major influence on his son's life and career. This influence began in the earliest years of John's life.

Born on December 12, 1892, John grew up in Oak Park, Illinois. He lived with his parents and five **siblings** in a house that his father designed and built. The house included a large playroom full of building blocks.

FUN FACT

One of the most famous buildings designed by Frank Lloyd Wright is The Guggenheim Museum. It is located in New York City and structured around a **spiraling** concrete ramp.

The Illinois home John Lloyd Wright grew up in is now open to the public for tours.

John's mother, Catherine, took charge of her children's early education. Both she and Frank encouraged their kids to play with building blocks as part of this education. The couple believed that building helped kids learn how to think and create.

Through building, John learned about shape and form. This led him to a career in **architecture**, just like his father. In time, John's passion for building would also make him a famous toy trailblazer!

Chapter 2

ARCHITECT
in Training

Wright was an **architect** for much of his life. But in college, he wasn't interested in architecture. In fact, Wright didn't know what type of career he wanted to pursue. As a student at the University of Wisconsin, he was uninterested in all of his classes. So, Wright left college and moved to the West Coast.

Eventually, Wright settled in San Diego, California. There, he worked odd jobs. He

San Diego in 1910, around the time Wright moved to the city

Wright drew plans for bungalows while at the Pacific Building Company. He also worked under Harrison Albright, a famous architect working for the company at the time.

also began to

think of his father.

Wright remembered the fame and social lifestyle his father had enjoyed as an **architect**.

Wright wanted that same lifestyle. So, he applied to work as a **draftsman** for the Pacific Building Company in San Diego. He was hired to sketch and draw plans for houses that would be built. Soon, he was promoted to chief designer.

Next, Wright applied to work at an architecture firm. At first, he mainly ran errands for the firm's owner. But in 1912, Wright was assigned to design and build a small home. Inspired by one of his father's earlier works, Wright completed the task. His next assignment was to design a hotel. With no formal architecture education, Wright was working as an architect!

Chapter 3

THE IMPERIAL
Hotel

Wright enjoyed working as an **architect**. He now knew it was the right field for him. So, he decided to receive formal training to increase his knowledge.

Wright wanted to **apprentice** under an architect in Austria. But when Wright told his father this, Frank invited his son to apprentice under him instead.

In 1913, Wright moved to Chicago, Illinois, to learn from and work with his father. There, he read books on architecture. He also took a class on structural engineering. Around this time, Wright married Jeanette Winters, a woman he'd met in California.

The Imperial Hotel was located near the Imperial Palace, home to the emperor of Japan.

After working together for a few years, Wright and his father took on a major project. In 1916, they were asked to rebuild the Imperial Hotel in Tokyo, Japan. The hotel needed to be rebuilt to withstand the earthquakes that often occurred in the country.

The Wrights worked together on the project for more than a year. Frank designed the structure around a system of notched timber beams that locked together. This would hopefully keep the hotel from collapsing in an earthquake. Meanwhile, Wright helped develop drawings and models of the hotel.

Chapter 4

A NEW PATH

Frank Lloyd Wright

okyo's Imperial Hotel was a dream project for a new **architect** like Wright. But Wright's working relationship with his father wasn't perfect. For example, Frank sometimes gave his son payments for his work. But he refused to pay Wright a steady salary.

In 1918, Frank asked Wright to collect money from one of his Japanese clients. Instead of handing all the money over to his father, Wright kept some of it for himself. Wright later told his father the truth. When he did, his father fired him.

FUN FACT

Tokyo's Imperial Hotel opened in 1923. The same day, an earthquake struck the region. But Frank's design withstood the impact. The hotel was one of few structures in the area that did not collapse!

The rebuilt Imperial Hotel in Tokyo, Japan

Frank continued work on the hotel. It opened in 1923. Wright hadn't gotten to see the project through to the end. But he had ideas for what he wanted to do next with his life.

While working for his father, Wright had begun drawing designs for toy construction blocks. His father's design for the Imperial Hotel had inspired him. The hotel's **interlocking** beams provided Wright with the basis for a grand idea.

Chapter 5

LINCOLN LOGS

Wright wanted to make toy construction blocks that were different from those he'd played with as a child. He **envisioned** blocks that were narrow and had notches at both ends. The notches would allow the blocks to lock together when stacked. This would make structures kids built less likely to fall!

Wright received a **patent** for the blocks in 1920. In 1924, his toy blocks were released to the public. Wright named the blocks Lincoln Logs after President Abraham Lincoln's childhood log cabin.

The original Lincoln Logs were made of real redwood. They came in a set for building toy log cabins.

The original Lincoln Logs box

Wright's Lincoln Logs **patent** includes his drawing of a completed cabin using the blocks. He labeled the cabin features and types of logs used.

CABIN FEATURES

1 Front wall
2 Rear wall (not pictured)
3 Side walls
4 Roof
5 Central doorway
6 Windows
7 Single window, rear wall
    (not pictured)

LOGS

8   Long logs
9   Shorter logs
10 Shorter logs
11 Very short logs
12 Semi-circular members
     or "half logs"

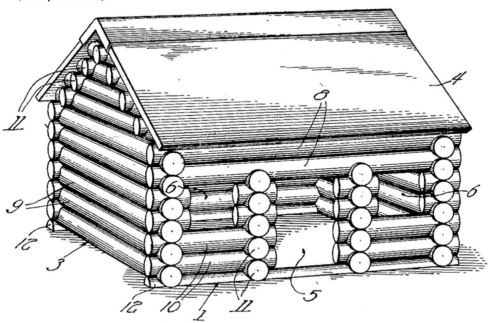

Chapter 6

SUCCEED
& Sell

Lincoln Logs were an instant success. Kids enjoyed building sturdy structures that looked like real log cabins. Parents liked Lincoln Logs too. They felt the blocks improved their kids' concentration and **coordination**. Between the late 1910s and mid-1920s, Wright designed other toys as well. These included chess pieces and toy animals. To **market** all of his toys, Wright started his own toy company in Chicago. It was called the Red Square Toy Company.

Despite his success in toy design, Wright remained interested in **architecture**. In the 1920s, he began his own architecture company in Long Beach, Indiana. By then, Wright was divorced from his first wife and had married a woman named Hazel Lundin.

Lincoln Stones were released in the 1930s and allowed children to build skyscrapers and other modern structures.

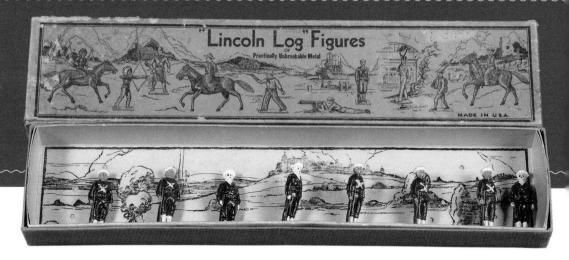

Wright's company sold small metal figurines made for play with Lincoln Log structures.

Throughout the 1930s, Wright continued to build homes, and his Lincoln Logs continued to sell well. In the 1940s, the United States entered **World War II**. This affected the American **economy** and many Americans' jobs. For example, Wright had been designing homes in Long Beach. But during the war, he designed a defense plant instead.

In 1943, Wright sold the Red Square Toy Company. Larger toy company Playskool bought it. After that, Playskool owned the rights to Lincoln Logs.

FUN FACT

Some historians say Wright received $800 in exchange for the rights to Lincoln Logs. This amount in 1943 is worth about $11,700 in 2018.

Chapter 7

WARTIME &
Wright Blocks

Lincoln Logs continued to sell well under new ownership, even during the war. But many toys did not. Common toy materials, such as metal and rubber, were needed to make war **vehicles** and weapons. So, the production of many toys stopped during the war. But wood was in less demand for war items. So, production of Lincoln Logs continued.

Meanwhile, Wright began a new chapter in his life. By the end of the war, he and Hazel had divorced. Wright then married Frances Gordon Welsh. In 1947, the couple moved to California and settled in San Diego. There, Wright continued his **architecture** practice. But as he built homes, Wright still had toys on his mind. He continued creating.

In 1949, Wright **patented** another form of building blocks called Wright Blocks. These blocks **interlocked** with one another like Lincoln Logs. However, Wright Blocks were more **abstract** and modern than Lincoln Logs. Their shapes allowed for building more **complex** structures.

Wright Blocks were offered in two sets. Number 1 Set had 36 blocks. Number 2 Set had 70.

Wright began selling Wright Blocks in 1950. But the new blocks proved to be more **complex** than toy buyers cared for. Wright Blocks did not have the instant popularity Lincoln Logs had.

Chapter 8

THE SPIRIT
of America

Wright Blocks failed to attract attention in the 1950s. But Lincoln Logs were reaching the height of their popularity! One reason for this was the baby boom. This was a period of unusually high birth rates in the United States. It began after **World War II** and lasted until the 1960s. Because more children were born in the 1950s, more parents were buying toys during this **decade**.

Another change in the United States in the 1950s influenced Lincoln Logs' popularity. More

Actor Fess Parker as Davy Crockett in the 1950s TV series

Marketing Lincoln Logs as representing the spirit of America is still used today! Many historians believe attitudes during the American frontier shaped the nation's modern culture.

and more American families were buying televisions!

Companies created TV advertisements to promote their products. Playskool took part in this practice, creating TV ads for Lincoln Logs. The blocks were among the first toys to be advertised this way. TV advertisements successfully boosted Lincoln Logs' sales. But so did the nation's growing interest in the **American frontier**.

During the 1950s, life on the American frontier was a popular theme on TV. The simple cabins built with Lincoln Logs fit into this theme. Lincoln Logs were **marketed** as toys that represented the spirit of America. This marketing approach worked! Lincoln Logs were more successful than ever.

Chapter 9

NEW VENTURES

Throughout the 1950s, Lincoln Logs sold very well. During this time, Wright also continued to design and build homes. Much of his **architectural** work was influenced by his father.

Like Frank, Wright practiced **organic** architecture. This meant he built houses using materials that fit naturally in their **environment**. In his California community, he primarily built with natural wood and **stucco**. Wright also began designing patterns for rugs and fabrics.

Although Wright had enjoyed **decades** of success in architecture, he still thought of toys often. In the mid-1950s, he decided to give the toy business another try. So, he made a **prototype** for yet another construction set. This new set was called the Timber Toy, and it was the most **complex** of Wright's construction sets.

Wright's Timber Toy included different shapes of **interlocking** wood blocks. It also included flat wood strips for floors and walls. Together, the pieces in a Timber Toy set could form a variety of structures, such as towers and bridges.

But the Timber Toy never made it beyond the **prototype** phase. This may have been because, like Wright Blocks, the Timber Toy set was too **complex**. Despite Wright's efforts to sell another construction toy set, he could not. His greatest success in toy design was behind him.

Chapter 10

HALL OF FAME

Wright's Timber Toy never made it to toy stores in the 1950s. But Lincoln Logs remained popular. In 1968, board game maker Milton Bradley Company acquired the rights to Lincoln Logs. It would manage the brand for more than a **decade**.

Meanwhile, Wright continued working as an **architect** until the end of his life. In 1972, he died in San Diego. He was 80 years old. Today, Wright's **legacy** lives on in the homes he built and the famous block toys he created.

FUN FACT

Lincoln Logs joined the National Toy Hall of Fame in the same year as the Hula Hoop, the Radio Flyer wagon, and the View-Master.

View-Master

A lot has happened to Wright's Lincoln Logs since his death. In the 1970s, Milton Bradley Company began making the toy blocks out of plastic instead of wood. This proved to be an unpopular decision, though. Lincoln Logs' sales declined.

Original Lincoln Logs were made from redwood only. Modern Lincoln Logs are made from several varieties of wood.

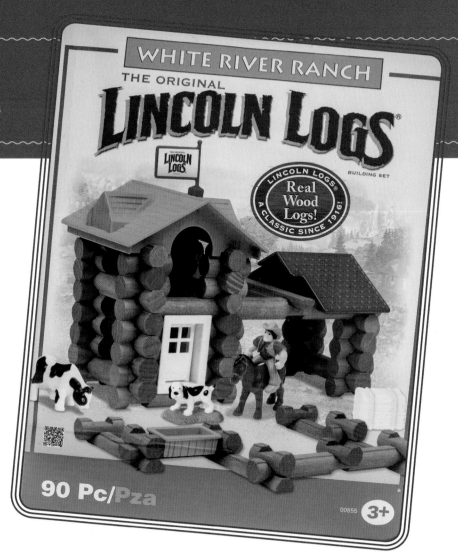

In 1984, toy company Hasbro acquired the rights to Lincoln Logs. Soon after, Hasbro brought back the original wood logs that previous generations had loved.

Throughout the 1980s and 1990s, flashy, battery-powered toys competed for kids' attention. Still, Lincoln Logs continued to sell. Then, in 1999, Lincoln Logs were **inducted** into the National Toy Hall of Fame! They had officially become an American classic.

Chapter 11

Made in THE USA

The same year Lincoln Logs joined the National Toy Hall of Fame, Hasbro licensed the brand to toy company K'NEX. Since 1999, K'NEX has been in charge of the production and **distribution** of Lincoln Logs.

One of K'NEX's goals **involved** the location of Lincoln Logs' manufacturing. Although originally made in the United States, Lincoln Logs had been produced in China for **decades**.

Now, K'NEX wanted to bring manufacturing of these blocks back to the United States. In 2014, it moved production of the toys to Pride

K'NEX highlighted Lincoln Logs' new manufacturing location with a "Made in the USA" label on the toy's packaging.

Manufacturing in Burnham, Maine.

Polls have shown that most Americans prefer to buy products made in their country. Since 2014, K'NEX has proudly advertised Lincoln Logs as a USA-made product. This new status created a lot of positive buzz for the toy.

Chapter 12

Ongoing LEGACY

Today, Lincoln Logs still have a place in toy stores across the nation. Many adults have good memories of playing with the blocks as children. In fact, these adults help to keep Lincoln Logs popular! They do this by introducing the toy to their children and grandchildren.

New **versions** of Lincoln Logs keep the toy alive as well. In 2016, K'NEX released the Lincoln Logs 100th Anniversary Tin. The special set celebrated the century since Wright had his idea for the wood block construction set.

As an **architect**, Wright was influenced by his father and often compared to him. But,

Each Lincoln Logs 100th Anniversary Tin included 111 blocks.

Many people consider Wright's Lincoln Logs timeless toys that will remain popular for a long time to come.

as a toy designer, Wright was able to forge his own path and **legacy**.

Wright's simple, notched building blocks have inspired kids to play with shape and form for **decades**. Lincoln Logs changed toy construction sets forever. And, they brought Wright's love of **architecture** into millions of homes!

TIMELINE

1892
John Lloyd Wright is born in Oak Park, Illinois.

1924
Lincoln Logs are released to the public. They come in a set with instructions for building cabin structures.

1950s
Lincoln Logs reach the height of their popularity thanks to the baby boom and TV advertisements for the toy.

1916
Wright and his father begin working on Tokyo's Imperial Hotel. The building's design gives Wright the idea for Lincoln Logs.

1943
Wright sells Playskool the rights to Lincoln Logs.

FUN FACT

Wright chose to put a drawing of a log cabin on the original Lincoln Logs box instead of a photo of the toy blocks.

1984

Hasbro acquires the rights to Lincoln Logs.

2014

K'NEX moves the production of Lincoln Logs from China to the United States.

1972

Wright dies in San Diego, California.

1999

Lincoln Logs are **inducted** into the National Toy Hall of Fame. Hasbro licenses the brand to K'NEX.

2016

K'NEX releases the Lincoln Logs 100th Anniversary Tin in honor of the century since the toy's creation.

Glossary

abstract – in art, expressing ideas or emotions without attempting to create a realistic picture.

American frontier – the geography, history, folklore, and culture in the wave of American expansion that began in the early seventeenth century and ended in 1912.

apprentice – to serve as a person who learns a trade or a craft from a skilled worker.

architect (AHR-kuh-tehkt) – a person who plans and designs buildings. His or her work is called architecture.

complex – having many parts, details, ideas, or functions.

coordination – the ability to move different parts of your body together well or easily.

decade – a time period of ten years.

distribution – the process of making something available to a number of people or different places.

draftsman – a person who draws or sketches plans for machinery, buildings, or other structures.

economy – the way a nation produces and uses goods, services, and natural resources.

environment – surroundings.

envision – to imagine or see in one's mind.

induct – to admit as a member.

interlocking – able to be joined or hooked together.

Booklinks
NONFICTION
NETWORK
FREE! ONLINE NONFICTION RESOURCES

ONLINE RESOURCES

To learn more about John Lloyd Wright and Lincoln Logs, visit **abdobooklinks.com.** These links are routinely monitored and updated to provide the most current information available.

involve – to require certain parts or actions.

legacy – something important or meaningful handed down from previous generations or from the past.

market – to advertise or promote something so people will want to buy it. This process is called marketing.

organic – related to or coming from living things.

patent – the exclusive right granted to a person to make or sell an invention. To apply for and receive this right is to patent something. A patent lasts for a certain period of time.

prototype – an original model on which something is patterned.

sibling – a brother or a sister.

spiral – to go and especially to rise or fall in a three-dimensional curve with one or more turns about an axis.

stucco – a material used to form a hard covering for exterior walls. Stucco is usually made of cement, sand, and lime.

vehicle – something used to carry or transport. Cars, trucks, airplanes, and boats are vehicles.

version – a different form or type of an original.

World War II – from 1939 to 1945, fought in Europe, Asia, and Africa. Great Britain, France, the United States, the Soviet Union, and their allies were on one side. Germany, Italy, Japan, and their allies were on the other side.

Index